Contents

PART I

A Reflection: *DOOMED FROM DAY ONE*...1

Too Damn Passive And Forgiving.......................................12

We Are All To Blame..............................17

Sacrificial Lambs................................34

PART II

Drugs Ain't the Answer...........................38

Zero Tolerance...................................48

RACISM Y2K: A NEW ERA...................69

About The Book

This book takes a look at Blacks in America and Black culture. And granted it does not speak for all socio-economic classes of Blacks, it is focused on those of us who have and/or disregarded or shamed the Black race and those racist Whites who have all but tainted it, and or destroyed it. Moreover, it is an overview of how we have gone from a society and culture that was once full of inspiration and hope to one of confusion and disgrace.

It was not necessary to do research. One only has to take a look at his or her surroundings and the like, to see how we have gone from being stable culturally and socially to a state of "critical condition."

There is no need to bombard the reader with stats as life experiences tell the story.

So, I invite the reader to take a look and see what how life, values, and morals have changed for the worse. Feel free to question and even disagree. But I can all but **GURAN-DAMN-TEE** that it will make you take a close look at Black America and our state of affairs.

Acknowledgement

To the brothas and sistas who understand the need to be militant and also say to hell with being politically correct!!!!

In memory of:

Mr. Yusef Hawkins

&

Mr. James Byrd, Jr.

Introduction

The Black experience has a mystique that is to be envied by members of other races and admired by those of us who live it in and live it with self-respect etc.

However, for too long the mystique has been tarnished and put to shame by Black-on-Black crime, babies having babies, *Brotha Sellouts and **Sista Sellouts and a host of other disgraceful lifestyles an state of mind that has overshadowed the dreams of those who fought and died for our civil and human rights.

So many have lost touch and have never been in touch with the fact that our ancestors were treated and bred like animals; owned as if they were property; bought and sold at the White man's discretion.

As late as the 60's the price for civil rights was hell to pay…having houses bomb and crosses just because it was allowed; terrorized at will by white men hiding like cowards behind hooded attire that from it's appearance alone could intimidate the strongest Black man; having dogs allowed to attack like we fresh meet and hoses turned on us with high pressure water flowing that could take a grown man off his feet. Yes, we have lost touch with what had to be done so that we could have the opportunity to live ***THE DREAM***….It has all but went to hell!!

Sure, the books have been written, the stories have been told the stats have been documented…yet there is still room and another reminder need to send the message that we need to wake the hell up and understand that the fight for true freedom is not over. Moreover, at the rate we are going especially generation next, we are in for a trip to hell in the worst way. Now there are those of you who will the words of the **Ruffwriter** with a grain of salt. However, I suggest that you have plenty of pepper on the side!!!

So, sit back and take in the language and vibe of the *Ruffwriter* as I put in black and white.

***better known as "female" Uncle Toms**
****better known as Uncle Toms**

Of note-The term Uncle Tom originally meant a man of integrity.

A Reflection: *DOOMED FROM DAY ONE:*

*IMAGINE WHAT IT WASN'T LIKE....THE WHITE MAN HAD LANDED ALONG THE SHORES OF AFRICA AND SHOUTED: "HEAR YE, HERE YE....***We are rolling out** the red carpet for all who can hear my call: come aboard as ships are sailing to the **NEW-FOUND-LAND***!!!*

Hear ye, Here ye, this is an open invitation to work hand-in-hand alongside the white man to build a great nation. We will grow and harvest crops, build bridges from coast to coast....for all your efforts each of you will be given 40 acres and a mule...

Some of you will hold offices such as president and vice-president. ...and your people will have equal rights in this land of liberty and justice for all" (LOL).

My Black brothas and sistas If you believe this bullshit...you have met one of the criteria's for being a "Brotha Sellout or Sista Sellout. And rest assured there are thousands of you who have lived and live in this fantasy world that America is the land of the free and the home of the brave.

Even since the turn of the century (Y2K), our civil and human rights are violated at the least. Inequalities on all socio-economic levels can be found from sea to shining sea.

OUR MOST POWERFUL BLACK LEADERS WITH A REAL CAUSE HAVE BEEN PUT TO DEATH AND AT THE CLOSE OF THE 20th CENTURY NO ONE HAS HAD THE BALLS OR SUPPORT TO CARRY THE TORCH.

In reference to leadership of this **UN-UNITED NATION OF PEOPLE**: If we play a numbers game, out of all the presidents in the U.S. **NOT ONE OF THEM CAN**

We are still blind to what this nation is built on: lies, deceit, and injustice for minorities, especially BLACKS.

Hear ye, hear ye…"my country tis-of-the, sweet land of liberty…." Hmmm....these lyrics were one of the biggest lies I ever recited when I was a second grader and that was damn near forty years ago and my race of people (Blacks) are still hearing the same old bullshit…get real!!!

Hear ye, hear ye…."I pledge allegiance to the flag of the United States of America…." Oops, that's for White America for the rest of y'all: they meant:

Now for the **REAL TALK!!!**- It is approximately 8,945 miles from Africa to the United States. Imagine traveling that distance by boat, packed in tight from the floor to the ceiling like sardines-air tight. What were the chances of making it to America **ALIVE???** Let's just say that it was not good. And for those who survived the journey from **HELL** their just reward was a life of **SLAVERY!!!**

◘ ◘ ◘ ◘ ◘ ◘

Since I was old enough to understand and appreciate what it meant to say: **"Say It Loud, I'm Black and I'm Proud,"** as profoundly stated in James Brown's song and title, there has been a serious breakdown and shakeup in both social and cultural conditions and now there is almost nothing left to be proud of.

The image and the lifestyle of Blacks have all but gone to hell and are steadily declining. Back in the day, the image was not spotless but it surely had some glimmer of dignity. It was all about the betterment of Blacks as a whole. Now the image that the media and entertainment world wanted the public to see was a far cry in my estimation compared to what we see today in real life and on the big screen.

Some believe that you have to go back to slavery to understand why we have that slave mentality. That may be true but I believe that for the most part it is not necessary to refer to slavery, to see how the morals, values, and the like of many Blacks have gone to the dogs. We must keep in mind that things have only gone all to hell over the last 10-15 years. One need only analyze the way of life from the '70s to the present to get the whole story in my estimation.

In looking back over a thirty-five year period, 1965-1999, it is disheartening to see the dramatic changes within our Black community.

At the close of the '60s the communities were close knit, neighbors looked out for one another, our children, and our homes. Parents and teachers kept us in check and made sure that no one bothered us. We shared what we had no matter how much or how little. Social bonds were definitely strong. Neighbors were not stealing from one another and surely were not killing one another at the rate we are doing now. The difference now is that not only will your neighbor kill or rob you, as one comedian said: "If they heard that your house has been broken into, they are the ones who have done it, but will come over the next day with a look of innocence and say: "I heard y'all got robbed." They put new meaning into the community watch program.

Despite single parent mothers being common, kids were for the most part well behaved and that was a blessing.

In the '70s we seemed to be striving as a whole to make a better way. Parents taught us to respect them and to respect ourselves; it was: "Yes Ma'am" and No Ma'am…Yes Sir and No Sir." If we made the mistake of saying Yeah or No, we were firmly reminded that we were being disrespectful and they put us in our place and rightfully so.

Our Black teachers were allowed to be disciplinarians and rightfully so. They did not mind tapping on that ass when we got out of line. Even, I was introduced to the black leather strap could inflict and believe me it made a statement.

It seemed as though the "problem child" was few and far between. Maybe it was the luck of the draw, maybe not.

I was exposed to teachers in the north and south and in both cases Black culture and history was emphasized. Most importantly it was the positive aspects of Black culture that was reinforced. We took Black movies with a grain of salt, that portrayed and upheld the Black pimp and drug dealer(s). In other words we saw those movies as entertainment for the most part.

By the time the '80s rolled in, things had changed. It seemed as though Blacks were no longer being spotlighted not even in a negative light. My former fiancés daddy said: "After Roots, they (whites) got tired of seeing us on the tube." He may have been right. But eventually Prince (although he has at one time claimed that he was not Black) has Blacks going to the movies again. For once, we were able to see a real life portrait of a Black superstar. Blacks were again encouraged to try to do something positive with our lives.

As the decade came to a close and the '90s took center stage, it was clear that there was a changing of the guard. There were subtle but effective notices that things were not the same. From the music to the big screen it was surely a time to take notice and it was enough to make me quote the late great Marvin Gaye and say: Mercy, Mercy Me…"

In the music industry, a select few artists realized that we needed to do something about letting babies have babies, but it was too late. Gangsta rap grew into a monster that has grown out of control not only because of the lyrics but because it became a way of life—literally.

On the big screen, **"New Jack City***"* was enough to break my heart and it was a reality check because it was becoming all too real in everyday life. But that was only the tip of the iceberg as "**A Menace II Society," "Boys N The Hood,***"* and "**Jason's Lyric***"* all told a sad, pitiful and truthful tale of how sorry and ruthless too many young Black men were becoming.

For many years it has been sad to see Black women crying when their "baby" has been seriously injured or killed whether the result of gang activity or doing something else stupid. Now, my heart is always saddened by the loss of life. But, I had to start asking the question to those parents who say: "Oh, my baby…my baby was a victim." Now if your baby had not been doing the wrong thing or watching the company he keeps, then your baby may still be alive. Or, you get those parents who are in total denial by saying, "No, my baby did not do

it," but they were well aware that the little monster they
created because they were not there when they needed
to be, or they have closed their eyes to what their child
has become, has turned out to be a thug or something
worse.

An Attitude

As late as 1970, Black men were strong in spirit and were willing to take a stand against prejudice, racism, and discrimination. We were tired of being pushed aside and walked on. The battle cry ***"BLACK POWER"*** was more than just words it was a movement; it was an attitude. As a child I thought that it was bigger than life. I admired for the most part the style, and attitudes of young Black men and women. They were proud of their heritage and culture. From the Black radio stations to the Black business, it was something special to observe to see how unity within the Black community was natural and a growing intangible.

In the 1980s the subtle but effective breakdown began. I was almost in shock to see how not only the "White Man" was destroying Black culture, but Blacks were, without realizing it, "selling out" and began to alienate Black culture and adapt and embrace "white" America.

Make no mistake, the media played a vital role in changing the minds of young Blacks and causing a decline in Black culture. The availability of cable TV was a big influence. Blacks began to embrace the music of white artists from those so-called R&B singers to Heavy Metal Rockers.

As a student at a junior college, I noticed one of my Black classmates listening to his headphones and when he paused to take break I asked: What are you listening to? He replied: "The Pet Shop Boys." I was speechless to say the least. I was expecting him to say that he was listening to Cameo or some other Black artists. Now I'll admit that every now and then one or two songs by white artist would slip through the cracks, but he had had the whole tape. Yes, times had changed!

One of my former co-workers became consumed with music by white artists and it made me wonder: What in the hell was going on? Yes, I'm fair by saying the type of music one chooses to listen to is to his or her own discretion but when it is done to a point where he or she alienates one's culture, I do get concerned.

The cultural breakdown/meltdown was in full effect. It was happening all around and there seemed to be nothing to stop it. The one "Black" radio station that had been on the FM dial for decades had been moved to AM. That was the beginning of me speaking out against the demise of Black culture. And don't get me wrong that one radio station was not perfect as there were DJ's that I did not care for because they had a bad habit of interrupting songs before they had played 90%. But I must say that when it came to catering to the needs of its Black audience it came through with flying colors.

A Way of Life

Once upon a time, listening to music by Black artists became a ritual. And despite the few wannabes (whites) who have the audacity to cross over, there was no substitute for music by Black artists—***PURE SOUL MUSIC* such as James Brown's *"SAY, IT LOUD, I'M BLACK AND I'M PROUD"*** that only Black artists could provide "us" with. Songs of hope an inspiration that we needed when times were tough. And even on those occasions when we did not have a dime in our pocket we could play or listen to songs that made us feel better and get by until that next paycheck was in our pocket.

In 1990 as I listened to the promo by one of its many Black radio stations that stated: "The music you grew up with…and the music that grew up with you." This was a true and effective statement. It made me realize how important being Black is and was. But so much had changed, and it was only going downhill.

By the close of the '80s and '90s, there seemed to be almost nothing left to be proud of. Gang banging, babies having babies, and Black on Black crime, and drugs (crack), had all but taken over.

Gangsta rap had all but taken over. Perhaps through no fault of its own, in some cases it has become an incredibly bad influence on our Black youth and it has grown out of control. To top it off, who would have ever imagined the music that what an artist rapped about perhaps played a role in their death or seeing the name of a record label called "Death Row". Rest assured, with Suge Knight in charge, it is not a name to be taken lightly.

It is nothing short of heartache to face the reality of the decline and destruction of what was once a proud entity and way of life. I sincerely hope that all is not lost to make things the way that they used to be.

It used to be that if a brotha had a dispute with another brotha then they would settle it with a good ol' back yard brawl. But now that seems to be too much trouble and a waste of time. Tempers are so short that no sooner than you blink an eye, the issue is settled with gunfire or other forms of violence. Something is definitely wrong with this picture.

What has become a comedy of errors is that an individual will kill another and say that he is doing it in the name of respect. But it would be better to say that he retaliated because he was disrespected. Perhaps one of my best friends said it best: **"It is better to let someone call you a punk and walk away than to retaliate verbally or physically and take the risk of having your life taken." Make no mistake the madness must stop!**

It used to be that a parent could discipline a child without repercussion but now the courts say that you can't do this: That's bullshit. Like Steve Harvey said: "My daddy used to knock me out…but I'm still here" And he's right. Parents and our elders kept us in line.

It is for certain that lawmakers need to wake up to the fact if you don't let parents discipline (not abuse) their kids, then parents and the community is going to have hell to pay and that is no joke. It makes me wonder if these so called decision makers have shit for brains.

One of my late aunts was surely creative. She could take something as simple as a washcloth and when she added water, it could inflict some serious pain when she struck me with it. Believe me she could use that thing with authority.

Back in the day even some of the white parents did not play. I paid close attention when my white male friends told me that their parents did not mind using the *Hot Wheels* racing track strip as a substitute for a belt…damn that sounds painful.

It is enough to make one want to cuss as the lack of discipline both physical and verbal that so-called parents fail to use because they believe that their "baby" should not be punished. A met a young lady who thought that it was cute when her four year old would retaliate when she spanked him. I told her that she had better put a stop to his retaliation because if she did not, he will be whipping her ass in the true sense by the time he is twelve.

Too Damn Passive And Forgiving

One of the problems that we have is that we are too damn passive and forgiving when it comes to addressing the behavior of racist Whites. Demanding better i.e. equal rights and equal treatment. We have become either too comfortable or too scared to rock the boat. The sad part is that we will raise hell with one another on the most trivial issues and will not band together when it is necessary.

It all comes down to taking a stand against the system and fighting the power.

Every now and then I hear Blacks speaking out, at the least in frustration about the things we are allowing to take place within the Black community. I overheard two Black women asking: "Would the "white man" allow a Black male to set up shop and sell drugs within the white community? No, he would hang his Black ass.
"Would we let the "white man rape our daughters without taking action?

"Would the white man let Blacks come into their community and let Black men use their women as prostitutes? No, hell no? Then why in the hell do we tolerate it from our own people?

In All Walks of Life

Some have said that too much is being made of franchises using Native American nicknames for their teams such as Redskins, Braves, and so on. It's really simple: If the Native Americans say that it offends them then that is good enough for me. It all starts with respecting the wishes of others. I can guaran-damn-tee you if there was a team by the name of the "**Washington Niggers**," we would be raising more hell over as was the case with the restaurant chain that went by the name of *SAAMBO'S*....y'all remember the term *BLACK SAMBO*. So I can fully understand why Native Americans are upset over the use of the name Redskins.

Schools such as St. John's, Univ. of Miami (Ohio), Marquette and others who have shown enough respect to drop such degrading and classless nicknames and the rest should follow suit. Those intangibles go a long way.

I find it less than amusing that Blacks tend to "glamorize" other races who have no love for us. To bring it home-when they admire Italians such as the Gambinos-one of the most notorious crime families in history; or they will call themselves Gotti or even name their dogs Gotti.

Legend has it that Gotti and other big name Italians were as racist as they came. The Italians even have their own term for Nigger and that is *moulinyan."

⬠ ⬠ ⬠ ⬠ ⬠ ⬠

It's a new millennium but a school like the U. of Mississippi still "sponsors" the confederate flag even through sports and has a mascot that is representative of a slave plantation owner. And it makes me wonder: "How in the hell can any Black person aside from an "Uncle Tom" or female

equivalent, let alone an athlete attend a college like this. It makes no sense. And now they have a Black head basketball coach to go with the confederate flag…go figure!!!

Almost fifteen years since former Indiana coach Bobby Knight began to show his true nature, Black players killed me when they said that they wanted to play for Knight so that they could be "disciplined" young men. Now my response is: If your sorry Black as does not have "discipline" by the time you have reached 18 or 20 years old then how in the hell do you expect to become disciplined later in life. **It sounds more like they wanted to be obedient to *Massa Lynch* and I'm sure that Massa was more than willing to put his "boy(s)" in his place.**

Perhaps one of the most inexcusable acts of stupidity occurred in the summer of 1993. A commercial artist for *AT&T* took it upon himself to have a monkey sitting in a tree talking on the telephone representing the continent of Africa. Now it does not take a genius to figure out what race of people that the monkey was representing. It just so happened that I was tutoring a student that worked for *AT&T* at the time. I raised my eyebrows when she told me that it was a Black man that created the ad. I was out-done when she said: "He did not think the ad would offend anyone." What in the hell had he been smoking or snorting?

I find it interesting how some issues only become important to us when they hit home. There was a time when we would all get involved especially when it came to protecting our kids and our neighborhood. But, now more often than not people seem to turn the other way. However, when it hits home, they come crying for help.

Perhaps there are many reasons why we look the other way or don't get involved for the betterment of African Americans. Perhaps it is burnout. In years past—

boycotts, marches, and sit-ins was the thing to do when we were being treated unfairly. But, of course that age-old discrimination still persist and there is no end in sight. To a degree we are like worn out and tired soldiers. In addition there are fewer soldiers and willing to go to war for the cause. And perhaps we simply wait too late—we wait until the damage is already done and by the time we put out the fire, it takes years to repair the damage if it is not beyond repair.

We do have a say in how the media portrays us especially in fictitious roles. It is up to our Black actors and actresses to say no and not play that degrading stereotypical role.

The *NAACP* had good intentions by requesting Blacks to boycott the new TV shows in 1999. **It is like calling the fire department after a building has burned completely**. From my perspective it started with a "small' but serious problem. Small from the standpoint Blacks were too blind to see what was to come. Serious from the standpoint the entertainment business was disrespecting Black men—only showing Black women with white men when they felt that it was "ok" to have an interracial couple on the tube. Not only was the entertainment world telling our young Black sistas that Black men are not worthy anymore but only a white man knows how to take care of a Black woman. It is those subtle things that we fail to notice that gets us in trouble and by the time we open our eyes it is too late. **We need to pay closer attention to the "wolves in sheep's clothing."**

Now, they have taken it a step further by putting all the Black shows on two minor networks. Soon we won't have any Black shows or better yet almost no Blacks on the tube.

In recent years, the emphasis has been: Buy Black. Ok I don't have a problem with that but I'm not going to buy from that brotha or sista who is not going to back his or her product, who is not giving good customer service etc. I've heard the stereotype complaints such as: "You can't give a Black man your business because; he will cheat you." But those same individuals can't tell me that Massa does not do the same. And even when Massa tells us that he does not want our business, we are still filling his pockets with money...***LETS WAKE THE HELL UP!!!***

We Are All To Blame

One of the great debates is the responsibility of the Black role models in the lives of Blacks.

I have to agree with Charles Barkley on the one hand when he said: "Parents should be the role model for the kids. That is true but let's face it, kids look up to others as well as their parents and athletes are in the public eye so therefore kids are going to be influenced be it right or wrong.

I'll be the first to say there are very few if any positive role models left. To my dismay we have lost some credible ones along the way. The "Queen" of track and field—the incomparable Flo-Jo (Florence Griffith Joyner) left us heartbroken. However we can smile again and say that "Mrs. Jones" (Marion Jones) gives us hope and inspiration.

The media has tarnished the lives of Michael Jackson and others. It is certain that it builds you up and tears you down in the blink of an eye; in this hypocritical society there is no margin for err.

In the '70s there is no question that the Black athlete and recording artists were a major impact in the lives of young Black males and females as I was growing up. People like Hank Aaron, the late great Arthur Ashe were phenomenal in the eyes of many and rightfully so. They were a ray of hope that we could not only survive in the white man's world but also beat him at his own game. The Black athlete has given so much to sports—bringing fans to, and money into the game in large amounts and yet even near the close of the century whites have given them their ass to kiss. This was very evident in the home run chase between Sammy Sosa and Mark McGwire in '98. With several games remaining, Sosa still had a chance to finish the season on top in a closer race, but as a radio talk show host pointed out, it was a race to number 62 which McGwire did reach first but the celebration was for their "great white hope." I will give the league credit for having the balls to acknowledge that Sosa was snubbed in the midst of the madness. The leagues efforts to make up for it was a moot point in my opinion as the damage had been done and even when Sosa reset the record when he hit homerun #66 there was little to no acknowledgment.

An acquaintance suggested that if Black athletes really wanted to "screw" America then they could do so by boycotting Olympic Games. I could not agree more. It would really send a message to White America that you can't win a damn thing without the Black athlete. Of course they don't have the guts to do it.

But today the Black role model is almost a disgrace. Too many times they have been caught doing the wrong thing at the wrong time.

Moreover, athletes are out of control. I'm burned out on hearing stories about players breaking the law and at the most being slapped on the wrist for bad behavior.

Some athletes have gone absolutely too far. Athletes have become problem children and it is time for the major and minor leagues to enforce a zero tolerance rule and stand by it.

I will give the NFL credit for finally ridding itself and teams of "problem children" like Lawrence Phillips It certainly appeared that he needed more help than the league was able to provide and hopefully he will receive it.

The once respectable sport of boxing surely should have done the same with Mike Tyson…but let's face it, this so-called sport has worn out its welcome with real sports fans like myself.

It is like a comedy of errors listening to Black fans of sports and entertainment. They seem to be so confused. I hear them bitch and moan about Black quarterbacks not getting their due, that there are not enough Black coaches and manager's, they bitch and moan about racism. But they still look for that great white hope. They will quickly identify with Jason Williams of the Sacramento Kings as White Chocolate" and will refer to actor Jim Carey as "That White Nigga." I'm willing to bet that these pitiful souls who do so don't stop to consider whether either person or their other great white hopes would not dare live next door to them. And, most importantly they give whites an open invitation to use the word nigger, freely and openly. Just to prove my point a white coach for an Ohio high school team made reference to a player who did not show up for practice: ***"THAT NIGGER DOES NOT WANT TO PLAY." To make things worse, some of the Black players had that Uncle Tom" mentality by saying: Ah, that's just coach." These young men do not realize that even though they think that some white's "may be down with us," but let's be real they are not one of us!!!!*** Come on people make up your mind, either you love Massa or you hate him.

      We all have to take responsibility for what is wrong within the Black community as eliminating problems starts within the home. And granted there are so many broken homes that are too many to count. But we still have to start within ourselves and take personal inventory and then determine how each of us can make a difference in the lives of youth.

      Even our own medium, the Black radio stations are to blame for our state of being. That's right!!! Just listen to the music that is being played. There are countless songs that promote degrading women, drug use, gang involvement or gang related activity and then the DJs have had the audacity to say stop the violence and start showing respect for your Black women and have even gone as far as asking what's wrong with our kids?

Now keep in mind they do have a choice, they can either choose self-respect or the dollar bills. In other words, they can play the music that does not degrade or play what appeals to the hip-hop crowd. And I still argue that what sold before will sell now and in the future—I'm referring to the ol' school music. No, it was not perfect but you damn sure did not have songs promoting violence and the like. And you damn sure did not have record companies called *Death Row*.

Now for those parents who say let the child make the choice at least teach them how to separate the entertainment aspect of the music from the message. **It's simple: Teach them not to practice what the lyrics preach!!!**

In the mid to late '90s I'll never forget listening to the radio and a DJ paused as he was beside himself after announcing that another Black youth had been killed in a drive-by shooting. I could hear the sense of helplessness and defeat in his voice as he said: **"Just because you see this madness on television and in the movies that does not mean that you are supposed to go out here and make it true to life."** It is for sure that we must to drive this point home to the kids or we will continue to have hell to pay.

On one occasion a former business partner of mine overheard me quoting the lyrics to the song **"I Got 5 On It,"** In her disbelief she said: "I know you are not listening to music like that!" I responded by saying: "I know how to keep it as entertainment and not try to live the lifestyle." Moreover, if I should hear my nieces and nephews listening to the song or singing the lyrics I will make sure that they are able to the same. Unfortunately too many people don't including adults, don't use their common sense and separate fact from fiction.

I can't count the number of times that I have heard Blacks say:" The white man is keeping us down." Now, let's be real about it. Sure racial prejudice and discrimination is alive and well within the workplace and other social settings. But we have to take a look at ourselves and realize that we have to continue to fight the power. Case and point: A young Black man told me that the "Crackers" (white folds) would not give him any money as he was standing on the corner pan handling. It was only moments after I had gone on my way that I thought: "What he should do is ask them to help him find employment; there is more than one way to skin a cat.

We have to go back to the ol' school. Instead of doing what it takes to survive (legally) some of us have become lazy and began looking for handouts instead of just a hand.

When will we learn? When racist whites let us know where they stand it is mind boggling that we (Blacks) do not get the message. It has been proven that white fashion designers do not want "us' wearing his clothes. So why do we continue to make him rich? You only have to tell me once that you don't care for me because I am Black and you can surely believe that these designers will never have to worry about me spending money on his line of clothing. It is sad to say that I still see Blacks looking for that "Great White Hope." When we continue to do this, then we always regress and the dream will either die or become a nightmare.

There's Got To Be a Better Way…A Better Way

To quote the lyrics in the song "Wanna Be A Baller" by Lil Troy: …*There's got to be a better, a better way…* to maintain some sense of dignity as we struggle to survive in white America. We have done everything but the right thing nine times out of ten.

In my estimation the future looks bleak especially for the majority of young Black men. Rapper "Shock G" A.K.A. "Humpty" said it best: "I'm in a rage (expressing disappointment in Blacks)…they (Whites) say we are like animals and we prove the right!!!" The last time I checked, gang participation had not decreased. Now I will give two rival gangs credit for trying to put an end to the madness in 1990 but it was short lived in part because so many other gangs or wannabe gangs emerged. One gang member gave a hall of fame answer when asked: Why call a truce? **His practical reply was: "I got tired of going to funerals."** One would think that his response would send a strong message but it was in vain. And I have to take my hat off to the media. For once they had the balls to air a commercial (albeit short lived) to try to convince Blacks to stop Black-on-Black violence. For those of you who may have missed it: the commercial showed a Black male—arms folded standing next to a white male dressed as a Klansmen—arms folded, with the voice-over saying: ***"IF YOU KILL A BROTHA YOUR NOT A BROTHA YOU'RE A TRAITOR."*** What happened to this much needed public service announcement? The public could not handle it. Before I had a chance to tape it, it was pulled. ***NOW THE INFOMERCAIL IS ONLY A RUMOR!!!***

Gangta Kooda McGruda & Klansman Kleager
now have the same agenda…**KILLING BROTHAS!!!**

Only two years later did rival gang members show the utmost disrespect by having a shootout in the cemetery? Now I will have to agree with a friend of mine when she said that they were dressed for the occasion and all that was necessary when it was over was to dig some more holes and dispose of the bodies…they did not deserve a formal burial ceremony.

An acquaintance of mine told me of a situation where a young Black man, age 13 at the most, was invited to join a gang. If he accepted he was assured that he would "be taken care of.' Now the question of the decade was: How did this gang plan to take care of him? The hall of shame answer: **"They would bury him with a gold plated pistol should he be killed as a result of gang related activity…*KISS MY BLACK ASS!!!* You can't do a damn thing for me when I'm dead!!! There has got to be a better way, a better way.**

Just as serious but subtle (in some ways), those fraternities that use hazing as a way of initiation are a disgrace. You know what I am refereeing to: those frats that will whip your ass as a pre-requisite to gain membership. The last time I checked, an individual's parents are the only ones who are supposed to whip your ass for any reason…hello!!!

To add insult to injury, it was only recently that I came to the conclusion that you actually pay for that ass whipping (that you could easily get for free) when you pay to pledge— which ranges from $500 to $1,500…*WAKE THE HELL UP!!!!! ANYONE CAN GET AN ASSWHIPPING FREE OF CHARGE!!!*

There is not that much belonging to a social group or any organization in the world. I touched base with a former co-worker about the hazing practice and I had no problem asking him what he did to pledge to his fraternity. I cut to the chase and asked him did he get his ass whipped. He beat around the bush but finally admitted that he did indeed get beat down. I responded by saying to him:" There is a time when you have to use common sense when it comes to being a part of a social group such as a fraternity or similar organization. Sure we all want to feel accepted and belong to a meaningful group but let's face it, I am not that desperate to be a member in exchange for being beaten. It will never happen

    WHO WOULD HAVE THUNK IT??? Not so long ago if you had a conversation with a stranger—a Black male— there was no condition or stipulation for exchanging pleasantries. Oh, how that has changed. You best believe that conversation comes with a dollar sign. What do I mean by this? Well, what I mean is that over the last five years more often than not when a brotha asks: Hey brotha, how ya doin?" And I respond accordingly. Now, more often than not the dialogue ends with: "Brotha, can you help me out? Or "Brotha can you give me a quarter or a dollar? Now I don't mind giving every now and then but lately these young men look as able bodied as I do, and there are times when I'm wondering why is this man not trying to get an honest job?

Second Class Citizens…At Best

For too long we have been under the illusion on where we stand—our place in society. But since day one (slavery) we have on been second-class citizens at best. There have been and still are subtle reminders of this:

1. The **KKK & other White supremacy groups** *STILL GOING STRONG!!!*
2. **Racial Profiling.**
3. **We are being dragged behind trucks and hung in trees.**
4. **Countless lawsuits alleging racial discrimination.**

But despite it all, many of us are trying to live in the "white world" with the illusion that we are exempt from the madness. Sure, just as during slavery you have your "good house niggas" and you can be best believe even they know their limitations. And these select few are poor excuses for role models.

The question may be asked: How do we overcome? Truthfully, I don't think that we can for the most part. Let's face it, we are in a country that we are not even natives of—having been brought over here against our will and forced into inhumane labor. And now over 200 hundred years later we find ourselves trying to fight mental slavery as we are in a country that is truly white America in terms of the decision making process. As a result there is no way that we can expect to fully adapt as we have always been fish out of water in a foreign land. But on the other hand we can improve on a bad situation but the clock has been ticking for two hundred years.

There should always be the hope and dream that one-day things will change. But that dream has all but diminished and is now a never-ending nightmare.

For over 30 years I have seen the heartache, emotional pain, and selling out that Blacks have endured, I can only shake my head as it has all been in vain.

Um, um, um…The disgraceful confederate flag. This tired ass issue should be a no brainer and be buried deep so long ago. But, it is not and I find that hard to believe. Some have said that we should leave it alone and focus on issues such as education. Ok, I agree with that but some Blacks fail to realize that letting that flag wave is still symbolizing that we can still have our civil rights violated, racial profiling and the like. Now I have also come to realize that until Massa takes that damn flag down voluntarily, then we are fighting in vain. If the flag is removed under "duress" then it still means that everything else remains the same. In other words, we still are more than likely to be under the same civil violations that I have listed and that is scary as hell!!!

There is no way that you can talk about racial equality bullshit to me as long as that flag is present anywhere whether publicly or privately.

I can only applaud the former basketball player who at one time refused to stand during the playing of the national anthem before a game. Rest assured I would never stand again. This is not the land of the free and the brave; it is the land of the harassed, depressed and oppressed if you are Black.

Those before me and during my era have seen our Black leaders murdered, our women used as sex toys, and young Black men become honorary Klan members (drug dealers). But yet despite it all there are Blacks that still believe we have progressed: ***THEY MUST BE ON SOME GOOD STUFF!!!***

We have done our token fighting with groups like the NAACP but they have only been a pacifier and nothing more.

We have a problem of not being able to break the habit and also feeding the beast. It seems as though we can't make up our minds—either we love Massa Lynch or we hate him, meaning that when we see whites taking what is "ours" the full lips, the hair styles (corn row), the Ebonics—half of us complain and feel threatened and the other half think it's the greatest thing since sliced bread. Again proving that the "white man' knows how to keep us divided…what a shame. Then we start bitching and moaning by saying: "This was ours first or buy Black."

I will be the first to say that there are some things that I will forever lay claim as being exclusively a part of Black culture and that includes R&B music and the like. I refuse to accept substitutes. **But some of us that do accept substitutes i.e. so -called blue-eyed soul by white artists are the same ones asking what has happened to Black culture…it's simple, when we mix with other cultures it brings in the true meaning of America being a melting pot. However, we come out on the losing end as *IT BECOMES A MELTDOWN OF BLACK CLUTURE*. Let's wake the hell up!!!**

Dr. Martin Luther King, Jr.—the man, his legacy, what he lived fought and died for, is something great in and of itself. But despite all that he and those that worked with him did for us: how have we thanked him in return? We have not thanked him, in truth the way we have regressed. It is as if we have pissed on his grave and called him a fool for trying to make a better way for Black America.

I recall when Massa "let" us have Black history day. We said thank ya Massa and was content. We raised a little hell and Massa gave us Black history week. No I have to give us credit—we raised even more hell and Massa gave us Black history month. Yep, Massa made damn sure that he gave us the shortest month of the year too…we are so content with it.

THE KING HOLIDAY!!!…If we are supposed to be equal then why is it so difficult for states like Utah and Arizona to observe the King Holiday. And although Arizona gave in, it was under pressure—**the threat of having the privilege of hosting a Super Bowl taken away. If I have to twist your arm and in essence bribe you to observe a holiday in honor of a Black man, then you are not worth a damn to me. It is another reminder that we are only second-class citizens at best.**

It was brought to my attention that it is only on the Black side of town that you will streets named after Dr. Martin Luther King, Jr. As he put it this is the white folks way of saying*: "THAT IS FOR Y'ALL (BLACKS), NOT FOR US!!!"* And I never thought anything of it but when I stop to think about it, and think of the cities that do have streets named after Dr. King, they are all in the Black neighborhoods.

Inter-racial dating and marriage will forever be an issue. Those Blacks that participate are called everything from an Uncle Tom to and "Wench." Once upon a time my grandfather told me that when he was growing up a Black man could not even look at a white woman as it could cost him his life. Every now and then I have pondered as to why Black men "turn to" White women. I came to the conclusion that some do it because they now have the liberty to do so. They don't **for the most part does not**

**have to worry about dying because he has chosen a
white woman to be his significant other.**

At least since my years in high school there was
great debate over what race queen Cleopatra belonged
to. I recall whites raising hell that she was a member of
the white race and my Black peers argued the point. By
the time I finished college the debate was put to rest. It
was not because of anything that was race related it was
due to the fact that historians found out what a "slut" she
was. And before I could blink an eye the white folks let us
have her and all but insisted: Hell yeah she is Black. They
didn't want to lay claim to having a "white queen" being a
slut, there is no way in hell that they would.

▢ ▢ ▢ ▢ ▢ ▢

*THE SAGA CONTINUES...*In the never ending
story of alleged discrimination by public establishments, it
is not earth shattering to hear about a "white owned"
place of business refusing to serve Blacks...however,
they did do us one better...at least we could sit down and
look at the menu...now, we it appears that we can't even
get our Black assed through the door....think about it.

It is fair to say that Black men get a bad rap or too
much blame especially when it comes to disrespecting
and mistreating Black women. Sure when one Black man
beats his woman or calls her every name under the sun or
is that deadbeat daddy...that is one too many. But what
irritates the hell out of me is when I hear Black women
say:" **If you want to be treated right you have to be
with a white man...*KISS MY BLACK ASS!!!***

White men are just as bad if not worse, when it
comes to disrespecting their woman. They are better at
doing their dirt under cover and the media is certainly not
going to publicize it and ruin that golden boy image. Now I

must say that we do not help our cause but much more of it is made than it should be and it is not fair. Now if a Black woman chooses to date outside her race, it should not be because she wants to diss the Black male. And for certain don't be that *sista sellout* and do like Whoopi Goldberg and suggest to your white knight to do "Black face" and sell out by saying that he was not making fun of you, and in the case of Whoopi—she is as Black as they come in terms of skin tone.

More often than not I have heard Black women criticize Black men for dating or marrying out of his race. I can only say that what is good for the goose is good for the gander, however to those brothas who chose to "cross- over" I say to them don't go digging in the trash. As one comedian said:" You see the brothas with the White girls that the White boys don't even want: *TRAILOR TRASH!!!* I will say to those brothas and sistas who wish to cross the line, if you do, by all means don't alienate the Black culture. Now some of those sistas, who are critical of the brothas, have crossed over themselves with the illusions that her "white knight" won't beat her or cheat on her…it's time to put that lie to rest.

There are times when even Massa Lynch will even tell us how foolish we are acting, but we still keep shooting ourselves in the foot.

A friend of mine called me one day, and I mean he was raising hell. What was the problem? He was upset about the reports of the Klan apparently sending a letter to one of the Black churches which read in part: ***"BLACK MEN!!! KEEP KILLING ONE ANOTHER…SOON WE WILL HAVE ALL OF YOUR WOMEN.*** I calmly told my friend: "There is no need of you getting upset, hell Massa Lynch is telling us the truth and for once he is doing us a favor, letting us know he sees how **confused and desperate** we are and that's the truth. Now one would surely think that this would be enough to open our eyes.

Come now, if Massa is trying to give us a wakeup call and we ignore it, everything we surely seems hopeless. And we are in a new millennium? ***ONLY IN CALENDER YEARS, NOT MENTALLY OR ON A CIVIL LEVEL.***

◖ ◖ ◖ ◖ ◖ ◖

SAME OL' MASSA LYNCH, SAME OL' SLAVES: "Massa :Lynch" brought us here on slave ships, put is in chains, beat us down, raped our *BLACK* women, and killed us when we got out of line.

After a while Massa Lynch set us free! No, no, he only took the chains from around our hands and feet. He had done all the damage. He enslaved us mentally, put us in a position to keep ourselves in bondage—his social and economic system is tailor-made to do just that and that may last for infinity.

Over two hundred years later we have gone into a deep sleep, doing Massa's work for him—keeping ourselves in bondage. And when Massa Lynch sees us getting out of hand he puts us in "our place" he does so without us realizing it.

Yep, Massa has maintained status quo as he still has his good house niggas, and they do their job well, he has more "puppets" than you can ever imagine.

At one time a friend inquired as to why I view shows that have discussions with white supremacist and the like. I responded that it is because I want to be aware as to what is on my enemy's mind, what he or she is up to and so on. I want to be knowledgeable at all times what their tendencies are at all times.

◖ ◖ ◖ ◖ ◖ ◖

For some time Blacks have called Atlanta, Georgia the *Black Mecca* of the South. One day while standing in the Five Points area in downtown Atlanta, a young Black man looked at me and said, "Man…this is depressing…my people are just out here wasting away." "This is only the *Black Mecca* in terms of numbers because we damn sure are not progressing in terms economics and/or controlling the decision making process." The young man was right to a point as there were select brothas and sistas who were just hanging round, being loud, and even firing up the funk However, there were Black vendors along the sidewalks selling products such as sodas, candies and jewelry And if you go up a few blocks to Woodruff Park the brothas were seated playing chess and it was great seeing people out lounging and having a good time.

At least all is not a lost as I have had the opportunity to observe the activities of Blacks in other parts of the downtown area. In a nearby park young and older adults hold chess matches and that is a productive activity. I have also observed individual talent, especially aspiring artist. The most unique talent being a young man by the name of "Hantastic Hands" who generates music by blowing through his hands. I had the chance to converse with him on occasion and he is looking for his big break. He really works hard at his craft. When I see people like him working hard to do something productive and creative, I don't mind giving them a few dollars.

Sacrificial Lambs

That's right, we have been sacrificial lambs since day one. We have been and continue to be used as examples and the sad part about it is that we tolerate it. We continue to let the "white man" use us as puppets, to be his good house nigger, that "Uncle Tom" and "Aunt Jemima." We have been made examples of and allow it to happen. **Have we ever considered what would have happened had O.J. Simpson been white, his late ex-wife and her friend had been Black...how long would the "circus" have lasted? How long would Blacks grieved in comparison to whites given the race of those involved? How much would the media have hyped the murders? I am willing to bet my last dime that the answer is not very long, perhaps a month if that long. Oh sure, you may have received bits and pieces of news here and there until a verdict had been reached but that is about all.**

As a college student taking an English course, one of my class assignments included reading *Huckleberry Finn.* I had heard mention of the novel in years past but never took it upon myself to read it for my own enjoyment. Nevertheless, I read the story and ran across a line or two that summed up our "place" in society then and now. A character (Aunt Sally) in the story was told of an accident that happened on a boat. She asked was anyone hurt and Huck Finn responded: "No ma'am, ***KILLED A NIGGER***." Now to think that we were not even considered humans then—19th century, we are not on the whole considered much more now as we have just stepped into the 21st century.—***THINK ABOUT IT!!!!***

It is the thoughts and beliefs of people like Richard's that are passed from generation to generation…stay tuned for more of the same.

To all of you sports fans, those of football in particular: "Would a Black man have paid thousands of dollars (if he could afford it) for Simpson's jersey and then set it afire to show his outrage over death of a Black women? *NOT NO, BUT HELL NO!!!*

Consider this: You spend 15-18 years instilling your ol' school morals, values, and beliefs into your child; teaching him or her right from wrong, and then your worst nightmare comes true. Your son has decided to join a gang without you knowing it and within a week is killed in a crossfire. Your daughter decides to date a gang member and he tells her that if she really loves him, she will show her love to all the boys. And when she refuses to do so she becomes that sacrificial lamb. Your child goes off to school but because DeMarco decides to get revenge against "Loracritia" he brings a gun to school and starts shooting and not giving a damn that bullets have no eyes and that being the case your son is killed and thus leaving school in a body bag instead of on the school bus. The horror stories are endless but one way or the other we have to regain control of our kids and give them the chance to live long and productive lives.

It was hard for me to face the reality that people especially young kids are dying in the name of respect or should we say disrespect. It was from a television show that was portraying life in the hood that I learned that this type of thing happens in real life. A brief scenario: A kid is going to be robbed of his shoes at gunpoint. In an effort to save his ass he runs. Of course he is gunned down. Now some time later the asshole that shoots him says that one reason he shot him is because the victim disrespected him by running...***THEY CAN GO TO HELL!!!***

As gang violence grew out of control over the last ten years or so, it was very disturbing to hear how innocent victims were having their lives changed or either losing them as a result. News reports of young kids getting caught up in cross fire; drive boys or being shot because of mistaken identity was enough to make anyone sick. It has gotten so bad that one reporter said. You can wear the "wrong" colors and as a result be mistaken for being a rival gang member. It used to be that if a young lady was walking to school or any other location with a red dress on it was not big deal, now it could cost the young lady her life.

For many years Blacks have been admired for being able to come up with unique styles of dress. It was not only the clothes that we wore, but also the way we wore them whether at work or play. However, in recent years I could not believe it when seeing young Black men wearing their pants and shorts and having them damn near falling off their ass. Whoever came up with this idea should be beat down. There is nothing appealing about this style of dress.

We have surely lost our way. And as a result we have fallen into Massa's trap of doing things his way without even realizing it.

Someone said to me: "The White man knows how to keep the minds of Blacks occupied so that we will stay in our place." This individual made reference to the home video game systems that had only began to explode on the scene in the mid-1980s. And yes, I was one of those victims who became a video game junkie instead of using the majority of my free time to become more educated. Like many Blacks I have paid the price for being a video game junky. Had I spent as much time in the library seeking knowledge as I did on the video games, I would be a lot more educated than I am no.

PART II

Drugs Ain't the Answer

Before using crack became the thing to do, marijuana use was almost as common as smoking cigarettes by the time I started my freshman year of high school in 1977. It seemed as if I was the only one that had not tried the "funk" by the second semester. I found myself literally running from the scent. One day during class there was a honey that sat next to me whose notes I needed to copy. As I leaned over to see what she had written on her paper as she held it, that funk that had absorbed into her fingers hit my sense of smell and I thought I was in another world. My girl had some strong stuff, I mean hall of fame.

"Gettin' cool" was not for me. But it seemed so commonplace and I could not believe it. One day between classes, a fellow classmate caught up with me and he had a big smile on his face as he said: "I found a nickel bag by the water fountain." I was not surprised or impressed that he had the reefa (reefer) on him but I questioned whether he found it. But. in any event he was pleased and I went about my business.

Our elders have been a cornerstone within the Black community. We have looked to them for guidance, to put us in check when they saw that we were out of line. Their words of wisdom and direction was something that we could respect and appreciate. But times had changed so fast before I knew what hit me. I was hanging out with a friend—a respectable kid for the most part. We stopped by his place and as I walked through the doorway the scent of the funk hit me. I could not believe what I was seeing—his parents were helping themselves to the funk. I politely told my friend that I would wait outside. I could only think: **"Something is wrong here: Parents are**

supposed to be setting the example and telling us not to use drugs and not use the do as I say, not as I do approach."

1986 was the year for everyone to receive their wake up call, to open their eyes to the potential dangers and destruction that potent substances can case. After a famous basketball player died from cocaine use, I **thought every crack pipe would have dropped to the floor in unison; I was sadly mistaken**. I could not believe that I was seeing such a talented young man, with such a great career in front of him had it all including his life taken away from him just like that. Visions of looking at his body being carried away in a body bag should have surely sent that message that ***DRUGS, ALCOHOL AND TOBACCO AIN'T THE ANSWER!!!***

JOINT DISSERVICE COMMITTEE

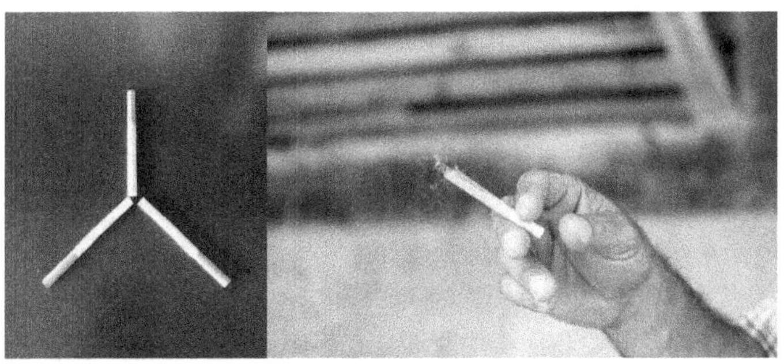

Cigarettes along with *marijuana are a large part of the drugs, and tobacco that are doing a disservice to Blacks.

*-Pixabay.com photo

It is sad that Black Americans especially did not take heed to what was going on, a **white substance** would terrorize a Black community or years to come and this is one instance when it is justified to say that: **"This White man (White substance) is what is keeping us down."**

This one death seemed to open the floodgates as it became common to hear that another Black life was taken away or destroyed via cocaine use.

I came to realize that one does not realize serious of a problem and how scary drug use is until you come face-to-face with it.

I met a young lady who was a beautician. This was during the time I was trying to get my hair to grow as long as I could. She and I made arrangements for her to do my hair and it was all-good as she was had competitive prices. About fifteen minutes after I had arrived at her home, she said that she needed to run an errand so I went with her. Supposedly she was going to pick up some hair products. As we approached the place to be, she suggested that I wait at the end of the block and she would return shortly. I did not see the writing on the wall. After some time had elapsed she called out to me to come to the place of business. Once I was there she said that I could come in. While inside, I saw more than what I bargained for. I mean there were drugs from *A to Z*, anything from the funk to crack and everything in between. To top it off the clientele was from the upper class: **doctors, lawyers, teachers and the like**. I could not believe what I had stepped into.

As I made my way inside the house dealer said: "You're cool." I'm glad he thought so. However, I was not cool emotionally. Reality set in as I thought: "I promise, if I am blessed enough to get out of here without incident I will surely be more careful. I must say the clientele felt right at home. I guess it was nothing for them to be there. As I was making my way to the door with ol' girl in front of me, I took a quick glance at the dealer preparing something that I did not even recognize. I knew that I had seen more than I needed to, and I could not leave that house fast enough. I thought: The entire social class of the Black community is going all to hell.

During the time I worked as a math tutor in the mid 90's I posed the issue of selling drugs to a student of mine when we took a break from studying. I inquired as to why so many young Black men like him chose this low life occupation. He said that in addition to the "glamour" an individual may have little or no education and may be in a situation where girlfriend is pregnant and he must find a way to support his child so what is he to do? Now I must say his answer had me dumbfounded. I did not have a "trump card" to respond with. But I had to respond with a respectable answer as I realized that this young man was considering selling drugs as an easy way out. I told him that selling drugs may be obtain "fast money" but you are surely taking the risk to a quick death; you are playing roulette with the lives others, you are killing your own people and to add insult to injury you are doing the work of the Klan with this ugly form of genocide.

His response what made me realize that we certainly have to come up with a solution to this problem.

And for the hat trick, in 1997 I had another encounter, I met another honey that I thought was on the up-and-up. So, I went to her place one evening and before I could get comfortable here comes her brother, in his teens, and he confidently indulged in the funk. I told Ms. Thang that it was time for me to be leaving. "Can I walk you to the bus stop?" I told her that it was up to her. As we walked in the direction of the bus stop she happened to see the community drug dealer and was going to make a purchase. Ol' boy noticed me and asked:

"What do you need?" My response was: "I don't need shit." I said it with an attitude and meant it.

In between all of that madness it was brought to my attention that in a neighborhood that I used to reside in there was a drug bust and to my surprise the ring leaders of the "drug circus" was an elderly couple with Jr. (a sixteen year old being the delivery boy). Yes indeed, "Grandma" and "Grandpa" even had better weapons than the police. **What in the hell is going on in our communities?**

The comedy of errors that I have experienced and heard tell of when it comes to drugs is sad. One thing is for sure, if there were ever any doubts to how serious of a problem drugs are and the possible consequences innocent people face, then they are taken surely taken seriously by me more than ever.

As time has passed my people have gone from smoking *reefa*, blunts, and using crack, cocaine, and ice (a form of meth).

Now I'll be the first to say that when it comes to knowing what is in the actual drug I do not stay updated the way I should partly due to the fact that I am not a user. But I also have wondered do drug users realize or even give a damn as to what is in their stash. A prime example is chronic. I had no clue as to what is put in this shit until recently. A friend told me that of all things it is made with **formaldehyde or if you prefer its common name**—***EMBALMING FLUID***. Now there is no way in hell I would want embalming fluid in my system whether I'm alive or dead.

It kills me when a brotha calls himself "helping me out" by offering me illegal drugs. They fail to realize that they can't do a damn thing for me if that is their way of helping me out.

Those encounters let me know that our community and our community is indeed in critical condition and we had better do something to turn it around

There was a time when I felt sorry for the drug user, the drug addict; I mean I really had sympathy for an individual. I was only finding fault with the drug dealer. But I came to realize that the blame should be placed almost entirely on the user. Let's face it—without customers—the dealer has no one to sell his or her product to. **And if anyone, I mean anyone is stupid enough to try marijuana, cocaine, and crack or any other mind altering substance available then damnit they get what they deserve because by now we all know what the consequences are and I have no sympathy for anyone whatsoever**.

If your eyes are still closed to how drugs have become our ultimate downfall, then here's another view:

Don't be like "Smoke Crack Jack": He's all cracked up!!!!

So all of you say your Black brothas and sistaa have been released from physical slavery. No big deal, White Power has taken on a new role and a new meaning.

White Powder has captured you and put you in bondage and will hold you longer and stronger than chains could ever do….White Powder speaks for itself:

"To those who have dared try and conquer me or escape my hold, I have tormented you mentally more than physical slavery could ever do.

"I have ruined your relationship(s) in every way possible. When you have indulged in my most potent form (crack-cocaine) it can and has cost you everything you own or was dear to you from your significant other, job, home, etc."

"I welcome those from all walks of life and social classes: doctors, layers, musicians, and athletes; I don't discriminate via social class. Bring me your rich and your poor and/or middle class.

"I am very sociable. I love parties, especially orgies. Threesomes or more…it doesn't matter."

"I demand loyalty and sacrifice from you…I want you to have me by any means necessary: "hook or crook."

"The only thing I can guarantee in return is heartache and pain to you or those that love and care about you. In short I will destroy you marriage. I will make you leave your wife or husband…oh yes, I go both ways….under-cover brothas ain't got nottin' on me."

"I have dared crossed the lines and joined the most sacred circles, the circles in your most beloved sports world." Want to know more????

        "I am credited with taking the life of one of the most celebrated athletes in 1986. Yes, credible sources insist that I was the reason he went from being a number one draft choice one day and carried out in a body bag the next...***I'M THAT DAMN RUTHLESS!!!***

        "From the way it looks, I can't be stopped. Not drug rehab, not education, not even seeing lives destroyed or lost has slowed me down...I will give your people some hope, let's say false hope: I challenge your people to prove me wrong ...time will tell!!!

Zero Tolerance

To reiterate: Back in the day we took a stand with marches, and sit-ins, protests. We made it clear to Massa that we would take a stand against prejudice and fight racial discrimination—even if it cost us our life. Now we have become so damn passive that it is a slap in the face to those who gave their all for us to get ahead.

No I am not saying that we should resort to violence that does not accomplish or resolve anything. But, I am saying that when Massa tells you that he does not want you to wear his close then damnit don't spend a dime on his shit. When a restaurant does not **voluntarily** apologize for insulting us then damnit make those bitches go bankrupt if we can. When representatives at Texaco made their degrading remarks you best believe some Blacks made a vow to never stop at Texaco for gas even if it meant walking 20 miles before they found another station other than Texaco.

For what it's worth let's live our lives and treat one another like we are in a new Millennium. It's time to progress people. Let's take on a new way of life by using ol' school values, morals and principles. It worked before and it can work again. Let's take a zero tolerance stance by not letting our kids disrespect us—demand respect and discipline (not abuse) them when they get out of line.

We have to teach and demand that our young Black men to respect our women and in return for the ladies to respect the men. And when someone like Ted Dansen pulls a stunt like "Black face" whether it someone else's idea or his own, we should boycott any show that he has a part in. It's time to take a stand and mean it.

To those young aspiring rappers, promoting the use of drug use, gang violence, and the verbal and physical abuse of our sistas is not doing us any justice.

The madness of babies having babies, there is no excuse. If you are going to have sex, then there is plenty of birth control so there is no excuse to become a parent before you are mentally and/or physically ready. And just to cover my ass. I am not condoning or promoting sex among minors or sex before marriage. I'm simply saying that if you are going to have sex then damnit use protection.

And finally, it is time that we quit looking for that great white hope, especially at the expense of Black culture. **At the rate we are going, Black culture will become a memory and perhaps a rumor**.

◖ ◖ ◖ ◖ ◖ ◖

Black Males, Who Gave Us A License to Quit???

For generations Black males have been held in bondage, both physically and psychologically. For generations our strength has been envied and feared. It has been envied to the point that the powers that be silenced two of our most powerful voices ever in Dr. Martin Luther King, Jr. and Malcolm X via gunfire, but who gave us a license to quit??? It has been feared to the point that we have and will always be a target by members of other races.

It is disheartening to say that some of us have turned against ourselves in the name of "disrespecting our manhood." We will go as far as committing murder to prove that we are a so-called man.

On any given day too many of us are standing at the corner with our liquor bottle when we could be educating our mind instead of killing your brain cells and liver….Who gave us a license to quit???

We stand at the corner and without shame or pride will ask for a nickel or a dime instead of at being at the employment office seeking work…**Who gave us a license quit???**

Many of our Black Queens are giving up on us as the number of "Undercover Brothas" and those who are open with their bi-sexuality are continuing to rise. Let's face it: they need and want and need a full-time man and not a *PART-TME PUNK*.

We have more degrading names for our Black queens that it seems like we are talking about dogs and garden tools rather than females; we find having a multitude of babies by a multitude of women to be a badge of honor rather than a badge of shame…Who gave us a license to quit???

We can emulate that rap/hip-hop star and recite his/her lyrics word for word but can't spell our name the same way twice….

Too many of us want to make big money the fast way so we sell that 'caine that kills our own race of people….Who gave us a license to quit???

Too many of us join that gang and are willing to pay the price even if the price is losing your life before you turn 18…Who gave us a license to quit???

Some of us have received that scholarship to attend a major university, excelled at sports, and the school made millions via our skills, but we did not attend class, thus we can't read past the sixth grade level, if we can read at all…Who gave us a license to quit???

Every now and then word on the street was: There are more Black males behind bars than there were free President Barak Obama stated: ***"We have more work to do when more young black men languish in prison than attend colleges and universities across America."***

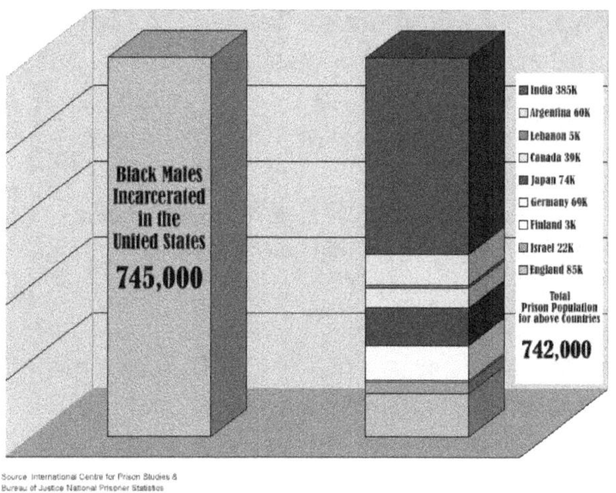

https://www.huffpost.com/entry/black-mass-incarceration-statistics_b_6682564

One educator told a group of kids: it is better to be enrolled at Penn State rather than the *STATE PEN!!!* Who gave us a license to quit???
We have seen and read the writing on the wall, just take a look at our so-called role models, especially those who double as athletes: **Read 'Em & Weep!!!**

Dexter Manley- He disgraced us all by allowing Oklahoma State to prostitute him as an athlete as he "completed" his eligibility but did not know how to read. To add insult to injury, prior to Washington vs. Buffalo in Super Bowl XVI Manley had the audacity to demand that questions directed to him be put in writing.

Magic Johnson-No one has to contract HIV or AIDS. May his experience for ever be the only warning we will ever need hereafter!!!

O. J. Simpson- I'll admit it was hard for me to believe that he could commit such a dastardly crime, but I had to wake up to reality. Perhaps he got too comfortable in his White world and now look at him…the hate that Whites have for him is staggering.
WHAT IF O.J. HAD BE WHITE AND NICOLE BEEN BLACK???!!! We know the answer to the question.

Ray Lewis- At the least too many brothas like him are guilty by association. Let's leave the hood and the boys in the hood state of mind behind when we have moved on to bigger and better things.

Rae Carruth- Too many brothas (and one is too many) are in relationships and love is not part of the equation …but for it to lead to murder is inexcusable.

Rev. Jesse Jackson- Having had a child out of wed-lock: We still don't understand that there is a difference between being holier than thou and being perfect

Michael Jackson- Since his initial problems with how he deals with children, discretion and common sense should somehow take over, but it looks as though it has not.

R. Kelly- There are plenty of women of age, who are more than willing to share in his lifestyle. It is a wonder that he is not pushing up daisies by now via a 12 gage because he has taken advantage of someone's under-age daughter.

Kobe Bryant- There were too many before him who had taken the fall for him to commit a "crime of stupidity". I can only ask: Did he not think for one minute that his indiscretion of being unfaithful would not go public???

Ricky Williams- Maybe it's just me (LOL), but when did smoking marijuana become more lucrative than an NFL contract???
They all have taken the fall and/or are **guilty** by association at the least of some heinous crime, crimes of law and crimes of stupidity….Who gave us a license to quit???
No one said that walking the straight and narrow would Nevertheless we have to look inside ourselves and rise again and be the positive driving force for our future of Black youth.

A BADGE OF HONOR? NO, A BADGE OF SHAME!!!

Somehow a "badge of honor" has lost its shine and is punching us a ticket to hell.
It has become a badge of honor for our brothas to kill one another in the name of disrespect.
It has become a badge of honor for our brothas to have child after child by one or more women and leave them to without a daddy.
It has become a badge of honor for too many of our brothas to be on the down-low and in return giving our Black queens HIV.
It has become a badge of honor for some of our sistas to become baby factories when they can't even take care of the first child.
It has become a badge of honor to degrade our Black queens and loving them to death via domestic violence.

The list is a short one but one of great concern….Moreover, the lifestyles listed is not a badge of honor it is a badge of shame—a low-down dirty shame.

BLACK MALES: REAL TALK!!!

I may ruffle some feathers but I really don't give a damn. The explosion of gay males and even worse **"UNDERCOVER BROTHAS" is mind boggling.** What happened??? And perhaps through it all is that any fall out directed at the "gay" community is directed at Blacks especially Black males. From my view, right in the ATL. Somebody thought it was alright to put up billboard for ALL to see that read: *IT'S OKAY TO BE GAY. JUST TELL YOUR WIFE….WHAT THE FUCK!!!??/ IT'S OK TO BE GAY….WHEN???*
As one radio personality once said, Y'all doing some NASTY SHIT…CALL *IT WHAT YA WILLL IT'S SOME PUNKASS SHIT ALL AROUND!!! I second that. WHAT THE HELL HAPPENED TO BEING A MAN??? …SOMEBODY HELP ME ON THAT QUERY!!!*

Black Females: Whatz Up Wit Ya???

My Black Queens, since day one you have been the gatekeepers of the Soul Generation(s). You were supposed to be taught to only allow those males into your life who were worthy of you love, and respected you to the fullest, and had something to bring to the table.
However, over time things have changed. You have forgotten what a real man is. He is not some who shows you "love" by leaving you battered and bruised, to say the least.

He is not someone who believes that if he can't have you, then no one else can.

He is or should not be someone who will be the death of you, but should be willing to die for you.

You have failed to understand that being a parent does not mean giving someone else the responsibility of taking care of your child while you go out and "shake that thang" and don't want to resume being a parent until you are ready.

You want the brothas to respect you although you use profanity better than a sailor.

Some of you have reversed the role of "boys will be boys" and now it's "girls will be girls" and have become the aggressor when it comes to learning about "sex education" outside of the class room before age 12.

So many of you criticize the brothas for crossing the line by dating outside of the Black race, but when you buy into the belief that "the only good man is a white man" you justify it come hell or high water whether it is out of love or not.

Sure enough as a whole we (Black males) have not helped our cause by more of us being behind bars than on the college campus, or worst case scenario killing one another like it's an epidemic. However, there are still enough good Black males to go around.

Mothers and Mammys.

Our mothers are cherished for the most part. They nurture and protect us until ware old enough to fend for ourselves. They teach us morals, values and self-respect passed down from generations past as only they can. When our daddies abandon us, it is our mothers who more often than not continue to support us by almost any means necessary that is legal. However, overtime mothers, have and are being replaced by mammys.

Mammys will give birth and leave child rearing to someone else, usually a grandparent. If that is not an option mammys will send the child to daycare and let those that provide the service be the primary care giver which includes love and affection. When the little tike is old enough they are raised in part by the television and in some cases in whole by the streets.

In short, mammys don't want to take the time to raise the child as they find to be too time consuming.

Mammys will allow their child to talk back or even hit them when they are in the midst of being disciplined. Mammys lose control by the time the child is two years old. Eventually their precious little baby is whipping the mammys ass by the time he or she is twelve.

Mammys will be the first to cry out: *"OH MY BABY"* when their *OUT-OF- CONTROL"* child pays the price when bad behavior has cost them their life or livelihood. Whereas a real mother will at least warn her offspring: *A HARD HEAD WILL MAKE A SOFT BEHIND.*

Mammys double as baby factories despite not having significant other help take care of the first one-three kids that they can barely feed or clothe as a single parent. *WAKE THE HELL UP, IF THE FIRST THREE MALES SAID: "I LOVE YOU," BUT LEFT. WHAT MAKES THEM THINK THE NEXT POOR EXCUSE OF A MAN WILL STAY FOR THE DURATION???*

The message has always been loud and clear. Children need mothers (and daddies) who are who are responsible. It is time for the gatekeepers of life to do the right thing and be a real parent…moreover it's time for babies to stop having babies.

THE BLACK COMMUNITY IS LOSING THE BATTLE TO PROMOTE AND ENCOURAGE MOTHERS TO BE RESPOINSIBLE. IT IS TIME TO TURN THE CLOCK AND TABLES BACK TO THE WAY IT USED TO BE.

OUR CHILDREN-GENERATION *NEXT IN TROUBLE???!!!*

Our children are our future. Like it or not we are all responsible and play a role in how they will carry on after we have passed them the torch.

Their innocence is precious and it should never be lost. Unfortunately more and more we have allowed our children to be exposed to adulthood before their time. We are exposing them to profanity, nudity, and other sexual innuendoes before they can read or write.

In reference to profanity, I've heard some parents say: I'd rather for them to hear it from me than for them hear it in the streets. Lost in this "logic" is keeping profanity out of the home then it won't hit the streets.

Our children are now growing up where parent relations are based on friendship as they are growing up with their parents due to the age gap being narrower. It is now become a question of who is raising who???

Actor/comedian Chris Rock put it in perspective: "You can tell who the bad kids are going to be when they are calling the grandmother mama and the mama Pam."

At the rate things are going how many more of our children will go from the womb to the tomb with the following sad story???

REACH OUT TO THEM!!! Over the years I go to the playgrounds where the young brothas are balling. I take time to ask them: How are you doing in school and what do you plan on doing after graduation etc. Sowing sincere interest and encouraging them is what we have to do for starters. After all, these are the young men who will be dating and marrying our young Black queens and having our young Black queens and kings.

Pixabay.com photos

If we don't help turn things around for our kids, then we may as well give them a cap and a noose.

From the Womb to the Tomb

As I grow and go from the womb to the tomb, my lungs are being body is being poisoned because my mother is a crack addict. I'll be exposed to cigarettes and/or marijuana to many times to count even before I open my eyes to the world.

This is what my future looks like: Instead of hearing nursery rhymes up to age five, my ears will have heard more profanity that my vocabulary will be filled with enough four letter words that will rival some adults.

By the time I start school chances are I will not know what a father is or even see a male figure in the house unless I have a brother.

I will know how to talk back to my mother and perhaps even have the audacity to hit back when I feel it is the right thing to do.

By the time I reach pre-teen years, I will have seen my female peers and adults put up with extensive verbal and physical abuse that I'll think it is a normal way of life.

I will know or become the drug dealer or user by the time I reach my mid-teens. Ya know I gotta walk in the footsteps of my homies and thus I will refer to hoes as females rather than garden tools…they have to know their place in a thugs world.

Now that I have reached early adulthood I don't know how to read but I can play football and basketball so the big name schools will surely give me a scholarship. …after all I gotta make it to the pros and take care of the ten kids I have here, there, and yonder.

Damn what I saw to be the future has come to pass…Look at me now!!!!

I'm in my twenties now. I had a damn injury so there goes my dreams of playing ball…what do I do now??? …Guess I'll have to compete for the business in the hood and slang that 'cane.

Man, ten more years gone by and ain't nothin' changed. I'm regretin' this shit and don't know what to do. My homies are either in jail or in the cemetery. This shit ain't right.

So much time has passed and I've become such a waste. Now in my late fifties I'm still hangin' at the corner. My homies that are left are just as bad off as I am, and now we have passed the torch two and three generations later. We are all competin' for the same corner, fightin' for the same dollar for our drugs and alcohol sales.

I can't believe it, time is winding down. Drugs, alcohol, drive-by-shootings, and gangs have torn my people apart. As I prepare to close out my life from the womb to the tomb let me leave by having at least tell those that walk behind me: "Walk a different path so that the journey from the womb to the tomb won't be so heartbreaking, filled with lost hope and tarnished dreams that was once filled with so much promise.

NIGGER OR NIGGA OR....???

We have had our own way of communication that is so impressive that even white folks have copied over since day one: What's Going On? What's Happening?; Whatz Up?, and so on. But in an effort to show one another respect and take a negative term and turn it into something positive does not always work. I'll never forget the time that a brotha boarded the bus and when he saw one of his homies he asked: **"WHATZ UP, MY NIGGA!!!"**??? My confused brothas and sistas mean well but there are times when we go too far to make an impression and this is not a way to impress any one.

ONE OF THE MOST COMPELLING WORDS IN THE ANNALS OF THE ENGLISH LANGUAGE IS "N" word "N" WORD. YEAH, YOU KNOW THE "N" WORD-- "NIGGER." A WORD THAT WHEN IT IS USED TO ADDRESS ANYONE, IT SHOULD BE REGARED AS BEING WORSE THAN OR EQAUAL TO HAVING SOMEIN SPIT IN YOUR FACE.

IT HAS BEEN USED TO DEGRADE, INSULT, AND OR ANTAGONIZE BLACKS/AFRICAN AMERICANS SINCE PHYSICAL SLAVERY WAS EN VOGUE AND EVEN NOW THAT MENTAL AND PSHYCHOLOGICAL SLAVERY IS THE NORM.

IN RECENT YEARS AND MAYBE DECADES EVEN BLACKS HAVE USED IT TO DEEM HONOR AMONG OURSELVES....HOW DESPERATE HAVE WE BECOME??? THERE IS ABSOUTLEY KNOW WAY THAT WE CAN TAKE A TERM OR PHARASE THAT ANOTHER ETHINIC GROUP HAS USED SO PRFOUNDLY IN THE NAME OF HATRED AND TURN IT IN TO SOMETHING HONORABLE....IT JUST ISN'T POSSIBLE.

NO MATTER HOW YOU DECORATE IT or as the late great Richard Pryor *once said when referencing ass hole:* ***"NO MATTER HOW YOU DRESS IT UP", IT IS NOT PRETTY: IT IS STILL THE N WORD AND IT IS TIME TO ELIMATE IT FROM OUR VOCABULARY.***

A MESSAGE TO THE WANNABE'S

It was my last year in high school that one of my teachers stated: We (Blacks) are the most innovative, creative and most copied (ideas) race of people. From our Ebonics, style of dress…the whole nine yards. And of course the main race of people that come calling are Whites.

So Whites wanna be down with us. It has been documented that it only takes 39 lashes from a whip to kill a man. So let's give 'em 38 (odds are, they will live) and then, whites can say: I feel and understand the pain and plight of Blacks…then *MAYBE* then they can say they are down with us.

The Confederate Flag

https://pixabay.com/

The confederate flag had flown in controversy at least since slaves were set "free."

To some of those from the old confederacy it represents a sense of pride and honor (these confused and ignorant souls that still believe in white supremacy etc.)

To others who are out-of-touch with U.S. history, they are indifferent as to whether it should be the flag of select Southern states or even represent the nation's flag.

From the time I was old enough to understand how offensive the confederate flag was to African Americans I was irate whenever one was in my view.

Given the fact that we will never be color blind when it comes to race and race relations my view of the confederate flag had changed stripes.

Let the confederate flag wave high and blow in the wind as long we are told that there is no racism and discrimination and covert racism is in full bloom.

Let it wave in red, white and blue until Whites understand that burying a white person's body next to one that is Black has no impact on the soul or spirit.

Let it wave until all men and women are treated equally and not just created equally.

Let it wave proudly and boldly until white supremacist, Klansmen, and Skin Heads denounce their ways.

Let it wave until Rodney King's plea of: *"WHY CAN'T WE JUST GET ALONG," COME TO PASS UNCONDITIONALLY!!!*

Let it wave until double & unwritten standards that separate the races are no longer practice.

Let it wave until future generations of Blacks no longer have the "Uncle Tom" syndrome.

Let it wave until there is a woman or minority president of the U.S. who is not playing the role of a "puppet."

"I pledge allegiance to the **CONFEDERATE FLAG** until racist whites denounce their ways...*"HEAR YE, HERE YE: WELCOME TO AMERICA!!!*

THE CONFEDERATE FLAG IS THE NATIONS REAL FLAG: LET IT WAVE UNTIL...!!!

RACISM AND SPORTS- SO YOU THOUGHT I WAS GONNA LEAVE THIS OUT???? THINK AGAIN!!!!! As with any way of life this is a bad mix and one that should not be in existence. However, we are still in denial that it is still an issue and even worse that it is a problem. So many times we have been given a wakeup call and are yet to respond or do not respond soon enough.

From the most notable to the almost forgotten stories, they still send a clear message that the sports world is not exempt from racism.

Although it was not made a big issue in 1978, The Royals Hal McRae claiming that teammate George Brett's batting title was white after he lost the closest race for the American league batting title due to a dropped ball by an opposing white player that was supposedly an easy catch.

And of course Unv. of Indiana coach Bobby Knight claiming that his Hoosiers would not have won the national championship game against Syracuse in 1987 had it not been for Steve Alford even though it was Keith Smart's (an African American) jumper that gave them the deciding pints….but racism does not exist in the world of sports…wake the hell up!!!

Sure Cincy's Marge Schott, the Dodgers Al Campanis and Jimmy "The Greek" Snider, and John Rocker of late were reprimanded but the "skeletons coming out of the closet," "the slip of the tongue," or "showing one's true colors" will not end with them. It is still the subtle actions that are still doing much damage because our eyes are closed to what is going on. The baseball looking to Mark McGwire as its *Great White Hope* during the home run race and chase of '98.

In 1992 Rodney King asked in part: **"CAN WE ALL GET ALONG???" THE ANSWER IS HELL TO THE NAW AND HERE'S WHY….**

As the 90s drew to a close, the history and hatred of racist whites was set in stone…So let's now put it all behind us by them turning over a new leaf. NOPE, it was not to happen come hell or high water. Instead, they chose to go out with a bang ….by dragging, yes dragging a Black man behind a truck to his death. **That Black man was Mr. James Byrd…*R.I.P.!!!***

RACISM Y2K-A NEW ERA

So, you that it would be fair to think that once the 20th century closed it would mean a new beginning for good race relations, "getting along," equal rights …the whole nine yards. Those who would even think such a bogus thought is still out of touch. Better yet as Malcolm X has been credited for saying*:" YA BEEN HAD, YA BEEN TOOK, HOODWINKED, BAMBOOZLED, RAN AMOCK.: WELCOME TO RACISM 2K!!!!*

William Bennett: And We Still Don't Get It!!!

So, we (Blacks) are surprised and outraged that former government official William Bennett in 2005 stated: "if you want to deter crime then abort Black babies"!!!!

His remarks are profound. I don't care how much humor he tried to put into it, there is no cleansing such toxic and racist words.

The question is when will we wake up and realize that views of Bennett's nature is are deeply rooted in White America and more than a handful of Whites. He "just happened to let them out of the bag.

We should not be outraged by his freedom of speech, we should be outraged that there are those of us who are still blinded by racism and racism 2k and that we expect White America to be free of racism…not in this lifetime and not ever.

Actually Bennett did us a favor. He reminded us that racism still has no economic or social boundaries and that Blacks are still viewed as second class citizens at best. It has been that way since we were "set free" and will nothing will ever change that mindset. It will always be us and them.

For good measure let us not forget that since day one we were not invited to the U.S. and the "red carpet" damn sure was not rolled out once we came ashore. We were literally taken and put into bondage, beaten like dogs, our women raped and killed at any given moment…just because.

We have forgotten that our ancestors were beaten to a pulp because "he" was reluctant to say his name was "Toby."

Yes, you sleepwalkers you have forgotten that at the close of the 20th century a Black man was dragged to his death in the name of *WHITE SUPREMACY.*

Have we already forgotten that no more than a month after hurricane Katrina that many Blacks were left to fend for themselves???

So be grateful that William Bennett said how he felt deep inside. Rest assured that he spoke for a fair share if Whites, if not he majority. Those with and without white hood and robes.

If we are upset with William Bennett, let it be because he tried to clean up what he said .and come hell or high water, there is no way that he can dilute such ***TOXIC and GENOCIDIC REMARKS!!!!!!!!!!!!!!***

AS FOR BLACK AMERICA WE STILL DON'T GET IT: WE ARE STILL VIEWED AND TREATED AS SECOND CLASS CITISZENS AT BEST.

KRAMER, KRAMER, KRAMER!!!!

In the '90s there was Ted Danson, Al Campanis, and Marge Schott and who could ever forget John Rocker????

Just when you thought that these cast of characters and their words of infamy could not be matched, enter William Bennett, and now Michael Richards a.k.a "Kramer" a character from the TV show Seinfeld. This is a short list of those that some naïve souls may never have imagined having such views of hatred, and anger toward minorities. . **They all have one thing in common: they let their *TRUE COLORS SHOW*. Furthermore, it is these high-profiled Whites who one after another answer Rodney King's query of "Why can't we all get along"????**

How we respond "Kramer's" racist outburst that somehow found its way into a comedy club will tell us a lot about ourselves and how in touch we are with racism etc.

Unless you have been away for a lifetime, one can easily detect a tone of hatred in his voice. "Kramer's" insults and such was not in humor and surely was not scripted. No apology written or spoken can excuse or make up for his defiant display of feelings that he expressed.

Of course there are the contingent of "Uncle Toms" and the like who will insist that we there was no harm intended and the wannabes who still don't understand that "being down with us" does not include the open and flagrant use of the infamous "N" word. **The "Brotha Sellouts" and wannabes can reflect on the words of their own "great white hope" Eminem and say: "Kramer was cleaning out his closet." He did a clean sweep.**

One good thing that came of this is that African American comedians Sinbad and Paul Mooney took the lead to make it clear that Richards' less than half-hearted apology is not acceptable and we all should feel the same. Moreover, the owner of the comedy club will not allow Richard's to return. Let zero tolerance be and stay in effect.

Let it be a lesson learned: those in attendance at the LA comedy club were expecting to see "Kramer," the fictitious character that they found to be entertaining on "Seinfeld"...what they got was the "real" Michael Richards!!!!

One might ask how could a man of Richard's social status etc. come out of the bag??? It's simple: here is a history lesson from a fictional novel

Don Imus...*NAPPY HEADED HO'S!!!*

Less than 5 months after Michael Richard's **TRUTH SERUM** showed us his real side, the sports world was rocked by Don Imus and his producer Bernard McGurick. There are references dialogue, and then there are references and dialogue. Image that your Black daughter is a basketball player on the college level and you decide to take in the game via radio. The commentators are Don Imus and Bernard McGurick, no big deal right? WRONG!!!

In the midst of the broadcast, somehow, someway: **HARDCORE HO'S** and **NAPPY HEADED HO'S** became part of the game description and analysis. *ARE YOU SERIOUS!!!!???* Yes sir, just as sure as I'm alive and well. Now, from the moment I heard about it, I was astounded to say the least. And I can only ask what could have gone through the minds of any one of those parents once that historic Imus/McGurck dialogue invaded their eardrums?

I thought: It's a no-brainer, the broadcasting careers of both jerks is over...*UH-AH!!!*
As the fall-out continued the one person who had a chance to defend the honor of the Rutgers' Black players was their head coach Vivian Stringer. When it was time for her and the players to meet with Imus she dropped the ball big time by saying that she was going into that meeting with an open mind....***WHAT THE FUCK???!!! GAME OVER!!! WE LOST AGAIN!!!***
***LET'S PLAY A NEW GAME...*A Black announcer is calling the action between two predominantly whits completion. One of them say's to the other: *THOSE ARE SOME BARBIE DOLL LOOKIN' WHITE BITCHES!!!* Rest assured they would be seeking**

unemployment in midst of the broadcast. *NO QUESTIONS ASKED!!!*

The hidden impact of what Imus and Co. did was and is everlasting as I can only wonder how many racist Whites said: *WAY TO GO DON…!!!*

De-Partying n Texas

Texas has a reputation for doing things big. This time it can be said that there are no limits as to how far they will go.

During the week of MLK day in 2007 at the least a few white students at a Texas university thought it would be no problem in mocking Blacks by portraying "boys form the hood, or "aunt Jemima." It was something seeing a young white girl wearing a read polka dot dress and a do-rag on her head. She had the biggest smile on her face that anyone would want to see.

It was another indication that the gap that separates "us and them" will forever remain.

The disgrace of it all is that some of the Black students accepted their apology and embraced them as if all was forgiven…There are those of us who still don't and will never understand that nothing has changed when it comes to racist acts

Donald Sterling

Perhaps Donald Sterling topped it all off with his racist rants that were secretly recorded. Sterling is a former owner of the NBA's L.A. Clippers who doubled as a racist S.O.B. How about his viewpoint of Blacks as he told his Black mistress: "It bother me that you want to broadcast that you associate with Black people and you can sleep with Black people, bring them in, but I ask you ***NOT TO BRING THEM TO MY GAMES.***"

Now, we all know that Donald had to go. The NBA would have no choice but to rid the league and sports of this ass hole. However, in the midst of it all the NBA dropped the ball. The decision was made to take a vote among the remaining 29 team owners-those in favor or not in favor of having Donald Sterling losing his control and privileges of owning the Clippers. Somebody saw the red flag that indicated any owner voting in favor of keeping Sterling would have to be in agreement with Sterling's views about Blacks......***THAT VOTE NEVER TOOK PLACE LADIES AND GENTLEMEN!!!!***

Divided We Stay Via Racism 2k

We continue to fail in so-called efforts to unite as a race of people....hell, we can't even find unity within our own race....we scatter like roaches when it's time to fight against racism e.g. the dragging death of Mr. Byrd in Texas by white supremacist as we showed up in small numbers and from what I could tell it was limited to the local residents...***FROM WHAT I UNDERSTAND MY PEOPLE ARE RAISING MORE HELL OVER MICHAEL VICK'S ISSUES (HE MAY BE GUILTY, I MIGHT ADD)***

THAN OVER WHAT HAPPENED TO MR. BYRD...GO FIGURE!!!!

Hear ye, here ye, it's a new millennium and we can hold these truths to be self-evident: *ALL MEN ARE CREATED EQUAL", BUT REST ASSURED ALL MEN WILL NEVER BE TREATED EQUAL.*

https://pixabay.com/en/photos/?q=kkk&hp=&image_type=all&
order=&cat=&min_width=&min_height=

One of the most intimidating yet **COWARDLY** sights in the annals of man!!!

AND BLACK LIVES MATTER???!!!

Black lives matter but we continue to have Blacks killing Blacks.

Black Lives Mater, yet *Brotha* and *Sista Sell Out* time and time again…in their eyes: **WHITES CAN DO NO WRONG.**

Black lives matter but we don't collectively hold ourselves to a higher standard. **HAVE WE NOTICED WHO THE BLACK ROLE MODESL ARE LATELY???** They include former and even current drug dealers and those with ties to gangs who are highly regarded. **WHAT THE HELL???**

A Black male who losses his head is like a body with no brains attached…that's what too many Black males have become.

Pixabay.com photo

Conclusion

With so many issues to deal with from so many angles, one has to ask: What does the future hold. It is hard to say in earnest. However, all is not lost as we have and will continue to have some great Black people in our talent pool. The question is how much influence will they have and how much control of the decision making process will we ever have to bring our people to a level of social and economic equality outside of the white world.

Let's be real, we have yet to have another Malcolm or Martin, not to mention a Black president (*NO PUPPETS PLEASE*).

From individuals to groups we have to initiate the winds of change….It's Y2k. If it they are going to start blowing then let the funnel clouds develop.

Up until the last two decades of the 20th century, there was still a glimmer of hope that we (Blacks) could and would overcome almost two hundred years of depression, oppression and suppression not only by the "white man" but also amongst ourselves but as a new Millennium has unfolded the future not only looks bleak but as songwriter/recording artist Lamont Dozier's lyrics say in part: "*…LIFE'S SO FRIGHTENING!!!*"

It is sad to say that Dr. Martin Luther King, Jr.'s dream has become a nightmare. We have some serious issues and the answers to solve and resolve them are very few.

I've only touched base on a few critical issues that are facing Black community and Black culture. There is so much more to the story. We need only walk outside our front door to see: What's going on. And I don't like what I see. It's hard to say what the future holds but it does not look bright. As a matter of fact it should scare the hell out of us.

Critical condition is our current status. Let's not allow it to down-grade to intensive care. We still have a chance to turn things around but time is of the essence.